D0172687

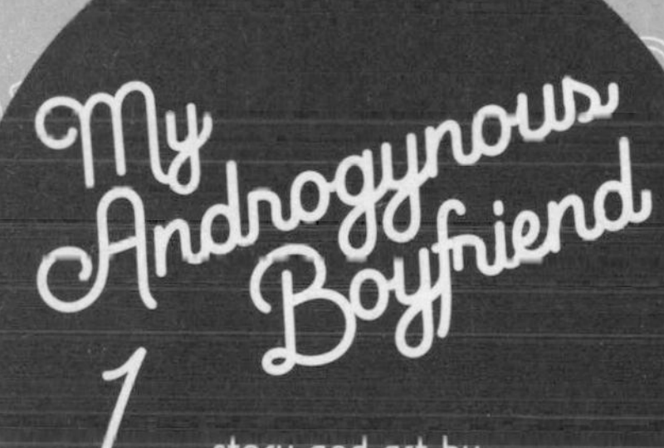
My Androgynous Boyfriend
1
story and art by
TAMEKOU

CONTENTS

The First One....... 3

The Second One....... 19

The Third One....... 35

The Fourth One....... 51

The Fifth One....... 69

The Sixth One....... 85

The Seventh One....... 101

The Eighth One....... 117

The Ninth One....... 135

The Tenth One....... 151

The First One

THE MAKEUP, THE CLOTHES, THE HAIR...

WOW! EVEN YOUR NAILS!

DOES THAT MAKE ME WEIRD?

My Androgynous Boyfriend
The First One

AN ANDROGYNOUS BOY?
I INTERVIEWED HIM FOR THE SPECIAL ISSUE. HE'S ABSOLUTELY ADORABLE!
AND HE'S NOT EVEN GAY OR A CROSS-DRESSER EITHER!
WHAT?! HE'S THIS HOT *AND* STRAIGHT?!
HE'S SO BEAUTIFUL. I'M JEALOUS!
YEAH BUT ACTUALLY *DATING* HIM WOULD BE KIND OF ROUGH.
DOESN'T HE MAKE YOU WANT TO SHOW HIM OFF?
......
THANK YOU FOR BRINGING THIS OVER.
NO PROBLEM. I'M HEADED OUT ANYWAY.
MHMM
THANKS AGAIN FOR ALL YOUR HARD WORK THIS MONTH!

DONE! IT'S FINISHED !!

TIME TO GO HOOOME !!

OH! IT'S MACHIDA-SAN FROM COMICS.

IS IT PROOF-READING DAY?

KA-SNAP

KA-SNAP

KA-SNAP

HAVE A GREAT NIGHT!!
SHE TOOK A PHOTO...
IS MACHIDA-SAN REALLY INTO *THOSE* KINDS OF CLOTHES?
THAT'S SUR-PRISING.
WAKO-*CHAAAN!*
OVER HERE! *HEEERE!*
チ公改札 Hachiko Entrance

YOU'RE FINALLY OFF WORK!
MEGURU-KUN...

YOU LOOK SO CUTE!
YOU LIKE THIS OUTFIT, HUH?
IT'S PERFECT ON YOU!
REALLY? THANKS!

I MEAN, THE FIT, OBVIOUSLY-- BUT THE COLOR, TOO!
YOU REALLY CAUGHT MY EYE IN THIS SEA OF DRAB WINTER COATS.
IT'S THE FIRST THING PEOPLE NOTICE WHEN THEY LOOK AT YOU.
HA HA HA! YOU'RE TOO MUCH.

I JUST GOT A NEW PHONE. HOW ABOUT WE TRY IT?
WASN'T TODAY YOUR PROOF-READING DAY?
I MADE A RESER-VATION.

WHAT? NO WAY!
THAT'S GREAT! LET'S GO!

TA-DAAA!
EVERY-ONE ON INSTA'S TALKING ABOUT HOW CUTE THIS PLACE IS.
CUTE.

WHOA! IT'S EVEN CUTER IN PERSON!
SO CUTE.

I FEEL BAD, BUT I GUESS WE SHOULD EAT IT.
SO CUTE.

CUTE.
CUTE.
KA-SNAP
KA-SNAP
KA-SNAP
CUTE!

CU..
ER, ALL LADIES RECEIVE ONE DRINK ON THE HOUSE TODAY...
OH!
THANK YOU SO MUCH!
OH, JUST ONE IS FINE.
UH?
WHAT...?
OH! MY APOLOGIES...
...

THE WAITER TOOK MY GLASS.

DIDN'T HE SEE MY LONG HAIR?

WAKO-CHAN...

SIGH...

I MEAN, IT'S PROOF-READING DAY. I ONLY HAD ENERGY TO DO THE BARE MINIMUM.

ANY OTHER DAY, I'D HAVE FIXED MYSELF UP.

I'M SORRY, MEGURU-KUN...

IT'S EMBARRASSING, ISN'T IT? HAVING SOMEONE LIKE *ME* BESIDE YOU...
WAKO-CHAN.
DON'T WORRY ABOUT IT!
I DON'T NEED ANY-THING LIKE THAT FROM YOU.
I DRESS UP FOR MYSELF.
I MEAN...
MY OWN BEAUTY IS MORE THAN ENOUGH!

YOU'RE RIGHT!

I SAW AN OUTFIT EARLIER THAT WOULD LOOK GREAT ON YOU!

ISN'T IT ADORABLE? WE SHOULD CHECK IT OUT LATER.

OH! I WORE THAT EARLIER TODAY.

WHAT ?!

I WANT TO BUY ONE! FOR MYSELF!
HEE HEE!
SHF
THANKS FOR CHASING AFTER ME, WAKO-CHAN.

HOW EMBAR-RASSING...

Q: Why do you put so much effort into styling yourself?

A: So the person I love can admire me when they see me.

The Second One
WAKO-CHAN.
ISN'T IT TIME TO GET UP?
IT'S MORNING.
UNNH. I DRANK TOO MUCH BEEER...
I KNEW YOU'D BE TIRED AFTER OUR DATE LAST NIGHT.
WE SHOULD'VE STAYED IN AND HAD A QUIET DINNER...
SHFF
コサ
SHFF
コサ
NO, I WANTED TO SEE YOU OUT OF THE HOUSE, MEGURU-KUN.

My Androgynous Boyfriend
The Second One
MORNING.

KISS
THE NICEST WAY TO WAKE UP...
KISS
KISS
KISS
RIGHT, IT'S LIKE...

KISS
ONE OF THOSE ALARM CLOCKS THAT GRADUALLY GETS BRIGHTER.
KISS
6:30
¥26,800
Roughly $250/US
KISS

AH!

I DON'T HAVE TIME!
I'VE GOTTA GET READY!
FWUP
EH?

TCH!
STILL BUSY EVEN AFTER ALL THAT PROOF-READING, HM?
WHY ARE YOU IN SUCH A RUSH?
I HAVE A MEETING AT ELEVEN!
I'M AT THE SHOP ALL DAY, BUT I'LL BE HOME TONIGHT.
WHAT WOULD YOU LIKE FOR SUPPER? I CAN MAKE SOME-THING IF YOU WANT.
WE HAVEN'T EATEN MUCH VEG LATELY. HOW ABOUT A HOT POT?
WE CAN CLEAN OUT THE FRIDGE.
HM...
WE HAVE MEAT. NOODLES, TOO.

brown
CLAMSHELL MUSHROOMS
white
white
BUT THERE'S NOT ENOUGH COLOR. EVERYTHING'S WHITE OR BROWN.
UDON
SUGAR
国産 豚肉こまぎれ 小
Domestic Meat slices
brown
white

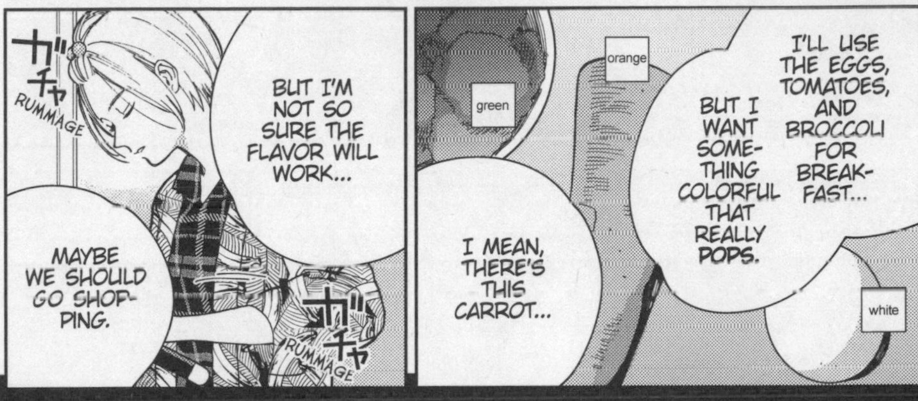
ガチャ RUMMAGE
BUT I'M NOT SO SURE THE FLAVOR WILL WORK...
MAYBE WE SHOULD GO SHOP-PING.
ガチャ RUMMAGE
orange
green
I'LL USE THE EGGS, TOMATOES, AND BROCCOLI FOR BREAK-FAST...
BUT I WANT SOME-THING COLORFUL THAT REALLY POPS.
I MEAN, THERE'S THIS CARROT...
white

BUT IF WE DO *THAT*, I'D RATHER MAKE SOME-THING MORE CHIC THAN HOT POT...
HRMM...
MY PRIMARY GOAL IS TO CLEAN OUT THE FRIDGE...

WAKO-CHAN

THIS IS SO LIKE YOU, MEGURU-KUN! I REALLY RESPECT YOUR ATTENTION TO DETAIL!

IT'S SOOO CUTE!

IT WOULD BE A CRIME TO EAT IT!

CAN I POST IT ON INSTA?

WHAT?!

YOU'RE STILL DOING YOUR MAKEUP?!

Mouth open!

WHAT HAPPENED? YOU'RE USUALLY DONE IN FIVE MINUTES.
THAT'S BECAUSE I WAS PROOF-READING.
TODAY IS MY FIRST MEETING WITH THE NEW ARTIST!
I'M A HUGE FAN!
I NEVER THOUGHT IT WOULD HAPPEN...
BUT I GAVE IT A SHOT AND EMAILED HIM--AND HE AGREED TO MEET ME!
Chocolate Nove
Kondo Kaoru
NOTHING VENTURED, NOTHING GAINED, I GUESS.

THE WOMEN HE DRAWS ARE SO SEXY! IT'S THE BEST.

IF YOU WANT TO TALK ABOUT APPRECIATION OF THE FEMALE BODY, THIS IS YOUR GUY.

WHAT? BUT ISN'T YOUR MAGAZINE FOR WOMEN?

RIGHT! EXACTLY!

DON'T YOU THINK A MANGA FOR WOMEN WRITTEN BY A MAN WOULD BE INTEREST-ING?

A MAN...

DESIRE...

Chocolate Nov

Kondo Kaoru

......

WAKO-CHAN!

LET ME DO YOUR MAKEUP.
WHAT?
YOU'LL BE GORGEOUS IN NO TIME FLAT!
OH! IT'S OKAY. MY PORES ARE SUPER OPEN TODAY.
IT'LL BE FINE.
AND I'VE GOT THESE LITTLE HAIRS POPPING UP.
I'LL TAKE CARE OF THOSE, TOO.
WHY IS MEGURU-KUN BEING SO PUSHY?
YEAH? I GUESS THAT'D BE OKAY...
OH! BUT...!

STAY AWAY FROM THAT LIME EYE SHADOW! I WOULDN'T BE CAUGHT DEAD IN IT!
SHUT UP!
スパパ
SWHUP
WHUP
パパパ
WHUP WHUP WHUP
……
OKAY. ALL DONE!
WOW!

My skin looks so different! It's glowing!

A genius!

You're amazing!

SQUEEEZE

Thanks, Meguru-kun!

YOU BETTER HURRY. YOU DON'T WANT TO BE LATE.

KOFF!

OH! RIGHT! SEE YOU LATER!

YEAH, YEAH.

I'LL CALL WHEN I'M ON MY WAY HOME!

NOW I'VE DONE IT...
I MADE HER TOO ATTRACTIVE.
EVERY-ONE WILL BE AFTER HER!
※Not going to happen.
BUT...
WAAAH!
I CAN'T DO ANYTHING HALF-HEARTEDLY!!

KA-CHAK

HUH? YOU FORGET SOMETHING?

YEAH.

BREAK-FAST!

GRAH
MNCH
MNCH
GRAH
MNCH
MNCH
GLUG
GLUG

PWAAH!

DELICIOUS AS ALWAYS! THANKS!
OKAY, I'M GOING FOR REAL NOW.

OH! HOT POT MADE OUT OF LEFTOVERS SOUNDS GREAT FOR DINNER! LOOKING FORWARD TO IT!!

WAKO-CHAN, WAIT!
HM?

MOUTH CHECK.
OKAY.
GOOD!
DON'T FORGET TO REAPPLY YOUR LIP-STICK!
FWUP
GOT IT!
BA-TNK
I'LL CUT THE CARROTS INTO LITTLE HEARTS FOR THE HOTPOT TONIGHT!

My Androgynous Boyfriend
The Third One

ARE YOU GETTING ENOUGH SLEEP, MACHIDA-SAN?
YOU MUST BE SO **BUSY** BEING A PROFES-SIONAL EDITOR AND ALL.

I GET ENOUGH SLEEP.
REALLY?!
WHEN I EMAILED YOU LATE FRIDAY NIGHT, YOU REPLIED RIGHT AWAY.
WELL, I'M IN THE OFFICE QUITE A BIT ON WEEK-ENDS.
I HAVE TO WHEN IT'S BUSY.
THAT'S ROUGH. YOU'RE A REAL TROOPER.

I WISH MY WIFE WOULD TAKE A LEAF OUTTA YOUR BOOK.
SHE ONLY WORKS THREE DAYS A WEEK, YOU KNOW?

BACK IN THE DAY, SHE WAS SLIM.
BUT SHE'S REALLY LET HERSELF GO.
YOU KNOW MY DEBUT BOOK?
Chocolate Nove
Kondo Kaoru
MY WIFE MODELED FOR THE COVER.
NO ONE BELIEVES ME WHEN I TELL THEM.
I GUESS I SHOULDN'T BE SURPRISED. SHE'S NOTHING LIKE SHE USED TO BE.
AND YOU KNOW, THE OTHER DAY...

UM, SO ABOUT YOUR NEW BOOK. I--
OH! LOOK AT THE TIME.
SORRY. I'VE GOT A DEADLINE WITH ANOTHER PUBLISHER.

ガラッ
KLATTA
LET'S DO THIS AGAIN SOMETIME. BYE!

I WANTED TO TALK ABOUT HIS NEW MANGA, BUT ALL HE DID WAS COMPLAIN ABOUT HIS WIFE.

COULD I GET A RECEIPT PLEASE? YOU CAN CHARGE IT TO MY COMPANY.

THWUMP

WAKO-CHAN, YOU'RE HOME.
YOU LOOK WIPED OUT AGAIN TODAY.
SO, SUPPER? OR DO YOU WANT A BATH FIRST?
OR--
I WANT YOU, OF COURSE. (HOT GUY VOICE)

KYAA!
KYAA!
YOU'RE DRUNK? SERIOUSLY?

RUSTLE
HM? WHAT'D YOU BUY?

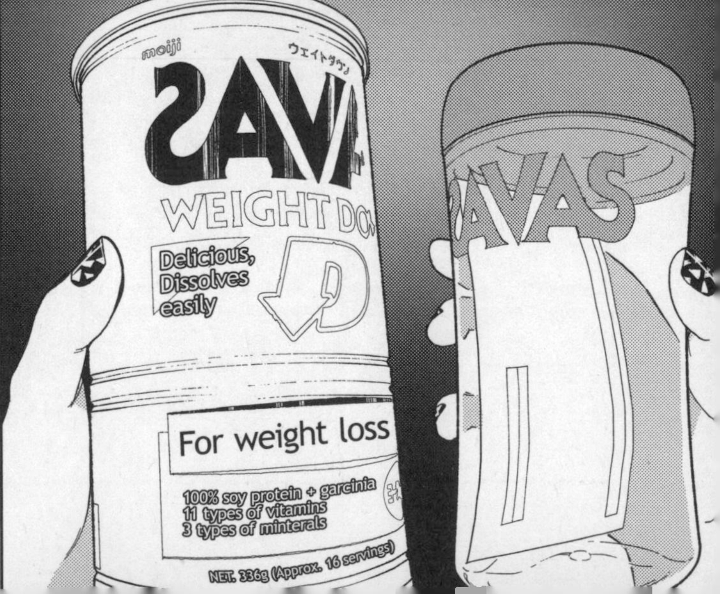
meiji
ウェイトダウン
Delicious, Dissolves easily
For weight loss
100% soy protein + garcinia
11 types of vitamins
3 types of minterals
NET. 336g (Approx. 16 servings)
SAVAS

WHY DID YOU BUY THIS STUFF AGAIN?
HEH HEH HEH! EXCELLENT QUESTION.

MMPH...
I'M GOING ON A DIET!

LOW CALORIE, HIGH PROTEIN, PLUS EXERCISE EQUALS LEAN MUSCLE!
I FIGURED I'D TRY IT FOR A WHILE.
WHAT?
WHY? YOU'RE NOT FAT.
I AM TOO!
THOUGH, I MIGHT ACTUALLY WEIGH LESS THAN YOU.

IT'S THIS EDITOR'S LIFESTYLE! IRREGULAR SLEEP! LATE NIGHT DRINKING!
UP ALL NIGHT! NOT ENOUGH EXERCISE!
I MIGHT BE OKAY RIGHT NOW, BUT I'LL GAIN WEIGHT IF THIS KEEPS UP!

I'M DOING SIT-UPS BEFORE BED!
HNGGH!
WOW... YOU'RE USUALLY NOT INTERESTED IN SELF-IMPROVEMENT, BUT YOU'RE WEIRDLY FIRED UP...

OKAY THEN! I'LL DO IT WITH YOU!
FASTING, GLUTEN FREE, SQUATS, RUNNING, WHATEVER IT TAKES!
OH! SORRY, I'M JUST REALLY DRUNK.
FWUMP
ぐだーっ
OH. C'MERE THEN.
PAT
ぽん
PAT
ぽん～
I DON'T REALLY GET WHAT'S GOING ON, BUT SOMETHING HAPPENED, DIDN'T IT?
YOU DID GOOD TONIGHT. JUST GO TO SLEEP. I'LL DO THIS FOR YOU.
BUT...
IT'S OKAY. DON'T WORRY.

EVEN WITH NO MAKEUP ON, YOU'RE SUPER CUTE, WAKO-CHAN.
THIS FROM THE MAN WITH INVISIBLE PORES.
SQUEEZE
Nngh! Ow!
I'm so happy, it's terrify-ing!

TO BE HONEST, I'M ONE HUNDRED PERCENT SURE YOU'D LOVE ME NO MATTER *WHAT* I LOOK LIKE, MEGURU-KUN.
I MEAN, I DON'T CARE MUCH ABOUT MY APPEARANCE.

SO WHY DID I SUDDENLY START TALKING ABOUT A *DIET*?
IT'S THIS LOAD I'M CARRYING.

DOING NEXT TO NOTHING WITH MY STYLE. AND ALL I DO ON MY DAY OFF IS SLEEP.
I WORK SO LATE, I BARELY COOK OR CLEAN.
AND SOMEHOW, A GIRL LIKE ME GOT SUPER-CUTE MEGURU-KUN.
THIS REALLY IS BLISS.

IF THIS WAS SUPPOSED TO BE AN EQUAL EXCHANGE, I'D HAVE DIED AGES AGO!

IF I DON'T PUNISH MYSELF, I'M AFRAID I'LL GET STRUCK BY LIGHTNING OR SOME-THING!

KA-SNAP

00:09

YOU CAN'T POST THIS!

YOUR EYES ARE HALF-CLOSED!

THAT'S WHAT YOU'RE FOCUSED ON?

YOUR FOLLOWERS SHOULD GET ALL MEGURU-KUN ALL THE TIME!

RETAKE IT! RETAKE IT!!

GRAB

O-OKAY.

TUG

HOW'S THIS?

GUOOI

She's always the one taking pictures.

KA-SNAP
OH!
GREAT! THIS ONE IS PERFECT!
HUH?!
UH, WAKO-CHAN?
AND JUST TO BE SURE...
DRAAAG
AHH-HHH!
JUST LEAVE THE EDITING TO ME!
I'LL THINK UP A CAPTION, TOO!
YOU CAN GO TO BED, MEGURU-KUN!
※CROPPING.

HUH?
HEY?
うおーっ
UWAAH!
WAKO-CHA--

ONCE HER EDITORIAL SPIRIT IS FIRED UP, NO ONE CAN STOP WAKO-CHAN...
UWAH...
GULP

FWMP

KA-SNAP

Likes 5,972

Yonto 1/5 Harajuku @yonto_harajuku
New today
We're totally into this sporty series!
POMA logo hoodie!
Meguru (@mmggling) and Papi (@yakiniku_v0w0v) are waiting for your visit today!
GIF
Twe
The Fourth One
THERE.
THAT SHOULD DO IT.
KA-CHAK
GOOD MOOORN-ING!
OH! RIGHT ON TIME!

OOH! SO MANY NEW ARRIVALS!
My Androgynous Boyfriend
The Fourth One

HEY HEY, MEGU-CHAN!
I GOT A LOT I THINK YOU'LL LIKE.
LONG TIME NO SEE, PAPI-CHAN.
YOUR OUTFIT'S ADORABLE AS ALWAYS.
THANKS!

I SAW THIS, YOU KNOW. YOU'RE A HOT TICKET NOW, HUH?
OH! YOU BOUGHT IT.

IT'S AMAZING! YOU MUST BE SUPER BUSY.
GUESS YOU'RE A PROFESSIONAL MODEL NOW, HUH?
NOT QUITE.
THIS SHOP IS STILL MY HOME.

KYAA! YOU HEAR THAT, BOSS?

WHAT IS THE MEANING OF THIS, MEGURU?

ずぉ~ん
LOOOOOM
I SAW YOUR INSTAGRAM POST YESTERDAY...

G-GOOD MORNING.
WAKO-CHAN TOOK THAT ONE...
AH HAH! I KNEW IT!

IS THERE SOME-THING WRONG WITH THAT?
OBVIOUSLY!
I MEAN, COME ON! YOU SERIOUSLY *CAN'T* WITH THIS PHOTO!

IT'S GOT "MY GIRLFRIEND TOOK THIS" WRITTEN ALL OVER IT!!
The editing's different from usual.
Weird angle at the left shoulder.
Cropping from the middle's off.
Posted in the middle of the night. A not-very-Insta-like background. ↓ A relative took it?

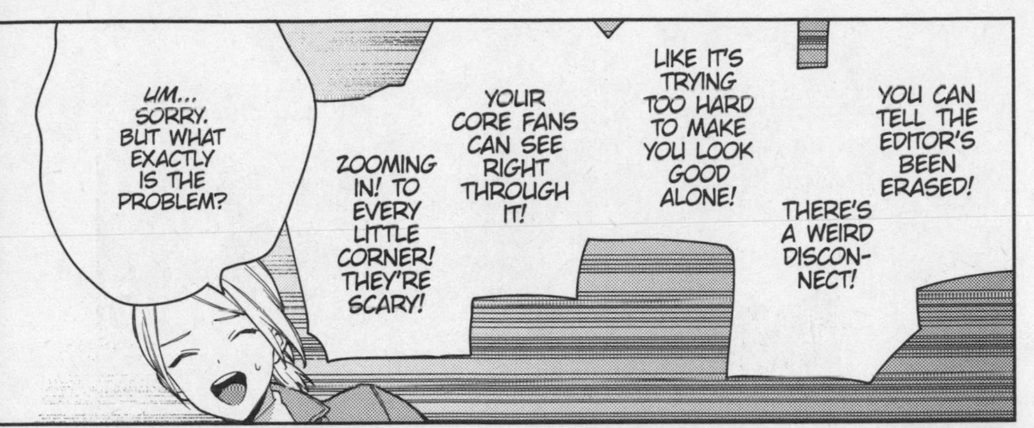

THE TALENT DOESN'T NEED A *GIRLFRIEND.*

LOOK AT THAT LINE! WE HAVEN'T EVEN OPENED YET!

CROOOWD

THAT GIRL AND THAT GIRL AND THAT GIRL OVER THERE!

EIGHTY PERCENT ARE HARD-CORE FANS WITH THEIR SIGHTS SET ON YOU!

YOU'RE OUR BILL-BOARD, MEGURU--AN IDOL!

KYAA!

KYAA!

THEY SPEND THEIR HARD-EARNED CASH BUYING CLOTHES LIKE YOURS AND THEY GET SELFIES AND SIGNATURES IN RETURN...

IF THEY FIND OUT THEIR IDOL HAS A *GIRLFRIEND*, IT'S ALL OVER!

THE DAY THEY LEARN THEIR MONEY PAYS FOR YOUR DATES WITH HER...

THEIR RAGE WILL BE HELL. THEY'LL DESTROY EVERYTHING IN THEIR PATH, AND BEFORE YOU KNOW IT, YOUR SOCIAL MEDIA WILL BE A WASTELAND...

B-BOSS...

KEEP OU

I'M SORRY.

THE BOSS'S BEEN KINDA BUMMED YOU HAVEN'T BEEN AT THE STORE LATELY.
SHE LOVES BRAGGING THAT YOU'VE BEEN WORKING HERE SINCE BEFORE YOU GOT POPULAR.
じ STAAARE ん
BOSS...
PAFF
I UNDER-STAND.
THE ME WORKING AT THIS SHOP DOESN'T HAVE A GIRLFRIEND.
OR RATHER...

The customer is my girlfriend.
I'll be everyone's Meguru!
SORRY, WAKO-CHAN.
THAT'S WHAT I WANT TO HEAR, MEGURU! YOU'RE MY BIGGEST DRAW!
LET'S GET THIS SHOP OPENED UP! PAPI!
ROGER!
DASH
WELCOM--
KYAA! MEGURU-KUUUN!!

YOUR SKIN'S SO NICE! YOUR CLOTHES ARE CUTE! YOU'RE SO PRETTY!
CALM DOWN--
PLEASE TAKE TURNS--
I WANT AN AUTO-GRAPH!
CAN I HAVE A SELFIE?!
LINE UP--

I'M SORRY, WAKO-CHAN.
I'M SORRY...
CROWD
CROWD
I'M SO SORRY!
ACTUALLY...
CROWD

HELP M--
EXCUSE ME!!!

I-I'M SORRY FOR YELLING.
UM, I'M IN TOWN ON A SCHOOL TRIP.
IT'S MY FREE TIME, SO I DON'T HAVE VERY LONG...
BUT I JUST HAD TO COME HERE.

THEY DON'T SELL CLOTHES LIKE THIS IN THE COUNTRY.
I'D STICK OUT IF I WORE THEM, ANYWAY. PEOPLE'D CALL ME WEIRD...
BUT YOU'RE ALWAYS SO CONFIDENT, MEGURU-KUN-SAN. AND CUTE. I WANNA BE LIKE YOU!

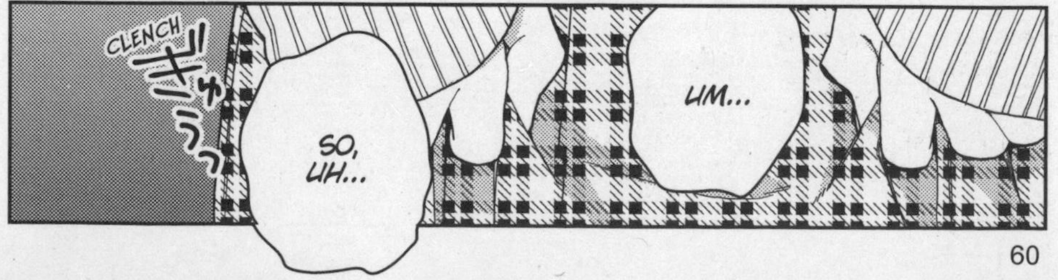

UM...
SO, UH...
CLENCH

I REALLY LIKE YOU! WILL YOU GO OUT WITH ME?!!

DID YOU CHANGE YOUR CARDIGAN'S BUTTONS YOURSELF?

AND YOUR BLOUSE ISN'T PART OF YOUR UNIFORM, EITHER.

IT'S CUTE!

OH...

UM...

I USED TO DO THAT, TOO. LITTLE THINGS THAT SLIPPED UNDER THE TEACHER'S RADAR.

THEY GET MAD IF YOU'RE TOO FLASHY--YOU HAVE TO BE SUBTLE.

THE LINING OF YOUR UNIFORM, YOUR SOCKS.

BUT I STOOD OUT ANYWAY. WONDER WHY.

I'M ACTUALLY SEEING SOMEONE ALREADY.
WHAT...?
SOMEONE TALLER THAN ME.
THEY EAT A LOT AND WORK ALL THE TIME...
AND ALWAYS TELL ME HOW CUTE I AM.

ALL EXCITED!
AND THE FACE THEY MAKE WHEN THEY SAY IT IS *ADORABLE!*
MEGURU!!
I'M SORRY.
IT'S JUST, I DON'T WANT TO LIE TO SOMEONE WHO'S BEING HONEST WITH ME.
I'M SORRY I CAN'T RETURN YOUR FEELINGS...
BUT I'M FLATTERED.
I DON'T WANT TO MAKE THINGS DIFFICULT, BUT THIS PERSON IS REALLY SPECIAL TO ME...
SO LET'S KEEP THIS A SECRET BETWEEN US.

OKAY?
AH...
UH...
UM!

THANK YOU VERY MUCH!

I'M DEFINITELY COMING TO UNIVERSITY HERE!

WHEN I DO, I'LL VISIT YOU AGAIN-- BUT NOT AS A FAN. I WANT TO WORK TOGETHER!

SO PLEASE STAY HERE, MEGURU-KUN-SAN!

I'LL ALWAYS, ALWAYS BE ROOTING FOR YOU!

IT'S OKAY IF IT'S A GUY.

Ginza
The Fifth One
SHWP
SHRRK
TAK
FWSH
TAK
TAK
TAK
TAK
TAK

My Androgynous Boyfriend
The Fifth One
HELLO? MEGURU?
ARE YOU FREE NOW? I WANT TO GET MY NAILS REDONE.

Tellus NAILS

HONESTLY ...!

YOU ALWAYS SHOW UP OUT OF NOWHERE, KIRA-KUN.

SO WHAT ARE YOU GETTING?
LET'S DO SOMETHING NEW THIS TIME.
HMM, I DUNNO. PICK WHATEVER YOU LIKE, KIRA-KUN.
SOME-THING PRETTY'D BE NICE.

IS... THAT SO?
YOU WANTED TO TELL ME SOME-THING, RIGHT?
UGH.
ANY-WAY, WHAT IS IT THIS TIME?
RIGHT...
EXACTLY! YOU ALWAYS GET IT, MEGURU!

I OVER-STEPPED MY BOUNDS AGAIN.
THE PHOTO-GRAPHER GOT ALL PISSY AND LEFT.
OOH, SOUNDS BAD.
I KNOW!
BUT I HAVE NO CLUE WHAT I DID WRONG.
IT WAS A BIG JOB, SO I WAS BEING MORE CONSIDERATE THAN USUAL...
"DON'T GET CARRIED AWAY HERE.
"JUST BECAUSE YOU'RE MORE BLESSED THAN MOST DOESN'T MEAN YOU AREN'T FLAWED..."
"THAT'S JUST HOW KIRA-KUN IS..."
IT'S ALWAYS LIKE THIS. WHEN I'M POLITE, I DRIVE PEOPLE AWAY.
I REALLY AM TRYING, BUT SOME-THING...
ALWAYS GOES WRONG.

ガタタッ
KLATTA
...

AH! I KNEW IT! HE IS HERE!
KIRA! THE MODEL!
HOLY CRAP! WOW!

I CAN'T BELIEVE WE'RE ACTUALLY MEETING YOU AFTER TRACKING YOU DOWN ON SOCIAL MEDIA!
HOLY CRAP! CRAP! CRAP!
UM... EXCUSE ME, MA'AM, BUT...
SERIOUSLY, I HAVE TO DO IT!
ドンッ
DUUN
AH!

TAKE A SELFIE FOR INSTA WITH US!!

GRUMBLE
AND I MEAN, EVEN BEFORE THAT... THAT, TOO.
I... SO THEN... IT WAS ALL... AND...
GRUMBLE
HE... SO... ......
GRUMBLE

K-KIRA-KUN, BEHIND YOU...
HM? BEHIND ME *WHAT?*
THESE GIRLS...
WHAT?

NOBODY'S THERE...
ANYWAY, SO... I DID... AND LIKE...
FOR ALL THAT... I MEAN...
PLEASE LEAVE...
K-KIRA!!

PIRON~!

OH! WAKO-CHAN!!!!

Wako-chan ❤

Where are you right now?

I'm getting my nails

want to see your new nails righ

Send a pic. Please.

Oh, I haven't taken off the

not that.

Send me a photo of you at salon, please

That's what you

The server took their picture.

HMMM?
I CAN'T TELL FROM *THAT.* FASTER TO JUST SEE THE REAL THING.
CALL HER OVER.
WHAT? ARE YOU SURE?
IT'S A CHANCE TO PROPERLY INTRODUCE US.
OKAY. BUT DON'T BE SHOCKED.
SHOCKED?

NGH...!
NGH ...!
HNNGH ...!
ガッ
THWUD

I WANTED TO PROS-TRATE MYSELF...
THAT'S A COMPLIMENT, RIGHT?
OF COURSE!

UM!
I'M PLEASED TO BE DATING MEGURU-KUN! MY NAME IS MACHIDA!
I'M AN EDITOR!
I'VE SEEN YOUR WORK EVERYWHERE FOR A LONG TIME!
I SECRETLY PRAY FOR YOUR SUCCESS!
THEY SAY BEAUTIFUL PEOPLE BLESS THE EARTH SIMPLY BY EXISTING, RIGHT?!
IF GOD IS EVER ANGRY ABOUT OVERPOPULATION...
I'LL PROUDLY STICK UP FOR ALL THE BEAUTIFUL PEOPLE!
YOU'RE SO SLENDER AND STYLISH, KIRA-SAN!
IF YOU STEPPED ONTO A CROWDED TRAIN, NOBODY WOULD MIND!
IN FACT, THEY WOULD BEG YOU TO BOARD...
THE CHUO LINE DURING MORNING RUSH HOUR!

ぼや BYOOON ん
NGH ...!
NGH ...!
NGH ...!
HNNGH ...!
HAAH... HAAH...
HAAH.
SO. THIS IS MY GIRL-FRIEND, WAKO-CHAN.
SHE'S CUTE, RIGHT?

HER BOOBS ARE HUGE.

HERE'S THIS SEASON'S NEW COLLECTION.

UNH!

IT LOOKS FAN-TASTIC ON YOU!!
WAIT, WAIT. JUST CALM DOWN!
HEY! DON'T YOU THINK THIS SILHOUETTE IS A BIT MUCH?
RIGHT. FOR A JAPANESE PERSON, IT'S A BIT...
BUT...
IMPOSSIBLE?
MAYBE JUST ONE IN A MILLION?
IT LOOKS SO GOOD ON YOU!!

My Androgynous Boyfriend
The Sixth One
KA-SNAP
カシャ
KA-SNAP
カシャ
WHAT'S GOING ON? A FASHION SHOW?
KA-SNAP
カシャ
KIRA-SAMA IS A REGULAR CLIENT, SO...

SEE YOU, MEGURU.
AND WAKO.
HE BOUGHT IT.
LET'S GET TOGETHER AGAIN SOMETIME.
VROOON
ブロロロロ
THAT WAS A BLAST!
I CAN'T BELIEVE I GOT SO CARRIED AWAY IN GINZA.
I REALLY HAD TO WORK UP THE NERVE TO SHOW MY FACE IN SUCH A PLAIN OUTFIT, THOUGH.
NICE GOING, CHEAP CLOTHES AT THE TOP OF ZQZQ-TOWN'S RANKINGS!
AS LONG AS YOU'RE HAVING FUN, WAKO-CHAN--THAT'S ALL THAT MATTERS.
AND IT SEEMS LIKE KIRA-KUN NOTICED YOU, TOO.
IT'D BE NICE IF WE COULD HANG OUT A LITTLE LONGER NEXT TIME, HM?
NOTICED?
YEP!

AH!
HUH?!
WHAT'S WRONG?
HALT
YOU SHOULD ALREADY KNOW THIS...
BUT YOU'RE THE CUTEST AND COOLEST IN THE WHOLE WORLD, MEGURU-KUN!
WHOA!
THANKS FOR SAYING THAT AGAIN.
BUT YOU DON'T HAVE TO WORRY!
I DON'T WANT TO TAKE YOU FOR GRANTED!
SERIOUSLY?

HOW ABOUT WE HOLD HANDS ON THE WAY HOME?

KISS

IT'S TOTALLY FINE!!!!
AH!
OH!
OH! UH!

ARE YOU ON YOUR WAY HOME?

PERFECT TIMING. THE PAPERS I WAS GOING TO GIVE YOU--

HUH?! NANAMI-CHAN?!

HERE YOU GO!

LET'S GO OVER THEM AT THE OFFICE TOMORROW.

THIS, UM...!

SORRY TO HAVE INTERRUPTED!

SO YOU'RE DATING SOMEONE, MACHIDA-SENPAI?!

I JUST ASSUMED YOU WEREN'T.
I MEAN, YOU'RE ALWAYS AT THE OFFICE FIRST THING IN THE MORNING...
DID YOU KNOW, BOSS?
OF COURSE.
YOU JUST STARTED WORKING HERE THIS YEAR AFTER ALL, NANAMI-CHAN.

SORRY, NANAMI-CHAN. I WASN'T TRYING TO HIDE IT OR ANYTHING.
FROM PEOPLE AT WORK.
NO, NO! IT'S OKAY.
THEY'RE BEAUTIFUL AREN'T THEY? HER PARTNER'S ACTUALLY A MODEL.
REALLY?!

HEY! BOSS!
GOODNESS. YOU DON'T MIND, DO YOU? SHE WAS GOING TO FIND OUT SOONER OR LATER.
BUT WE CAN'T TALK ABOUT IT OUT-SIDE THE OFFICE...
SO THIS IS JUST BETWEEN US.
AND, YOU KNOW, THEY'VE BEEN TOGETHER FOR AGES. THEY LIVE TOGETHER. IT'S ONLY A MATTER OF TIME UNTIL THEY GET MARRIED.
Boss!!

HUNH. SO THEN I GUESS...
THAT MEANS YOU'LL MOVE TO SHIBUYA?
HM?
I THOUGHT YOU HAD TO GO TO SHIBUYA...
FOR A **SAME-SEX MARRIAGE.**
THAT'S WHAT IT SAID IN THIS BL I READ THE OTHER DAY...
OH...
YOU STILL HAVEN'T MOVED YET--RIGHT, MACHIDA-SAN?
FWP
WHAT?
I HOPE YOU FIND A NICE PLACE.
IT'S ALL ABOUT TIMING.
I-I GUESS SO.

OH! ONCE YOU DECIDE, PLEASE LET ME VISIT!
RIGHT. THE WHOLE EDITORIAL DEPARTMENT SHOULD GO OVER FOR A HOUSE-WARMING.
MEGURU-SAN WOULD LOVE THAT!
AH! HER NAME'S ADORABLE, TOO!
WILL YOU DO DRESSES FOR THE CEREMONY? OR WHITE KIMONO? THAT'S A TOUGH DECISION.
WOULDN'T IT BE LOVELY IF ONE WAS IN A KIMONO AND THE OTHER IN A DRESS?
HAWAIIAN WEDD
OH! I SAW A PICTURE LIKE THAT ON TWITTER. IT WAS GREAT!
BOTH OF THEM HAD RED LIP-STICK...
OOH, THAT MAKES A PRETTY PICTURE.
AH...
KYAA!
UM...
KYAA!
MACHIDA-SENPAI!

I'M TOTALLY NOT PREJUDICED!
I REALLY HOPE IT ALL WORKS OUT!
HEY, NANAMI-*CHAAAN!* WHAT IS THIS?
OH! I'LL DO IT!
TROT
TROT
GOOD KID, *HM?* HONEST.
ARE YOU SURE ABOUT THIS? SHE BOUGHT IT, BUT...
WHAT DIFFERENCE DOES IT MAKE? SHE'LL FIGURE IT OUT AT SOME POINT.

SMIRK
THIS IS HOW NEWBIES LEARN TO SEPARATE WORK AND PERSONAL LIFE.
WELL, IT DOESN'T MATTER EITHER WAY.
コポポ
PLUP PLUP
YOU JUST THINK IT'S FUNNY.
MACHIDA-SENPAI?
HM?
UM... CAN I ASK YOU SOME-THING?
HM? WHAT IS IT?
IT'S... IT'S KIND OF HARD TO ASK, BUT...
WHAT-EVER IT IS, IT'S FINE.

YOU'RE LIKE THE MAN, RIGHT...?

......
......
......

I... GUESS SO!
I KNEW IT!
IT WAS JUST TOO TEMPTING TO PASS UP...

My Androgynous Boyfriend
The Seventh One

WE'RE OUT OF SPONGES. I WAS THINKING ABOUT GETTING SOME NEW ONES.

AND IT'S MORE FUN WHEN STUFF LIKE THIS IS CUTE, RIGHT?

LET ME KNOW IF WE NEED ANYTHING ELSE.

I'LL BUY IT ALL AT ONCE...

IS NOW NOT A GOOD TIME?

Shirt: Shima.

WHICH IS TO SAY...

IKEYA!
IKEYA
Entrance

IT'S FAR FROM THE STATION, BUT IT'S *HUGE!*
THE CEILING'S SUPER HIGH! LIKE A WARE-HOUSE!
Soft Serve Cone
¥50
Frozen Yogurt
¥180
THE ICE CREAM'S SO CHEAP!!
SEE? LOOK AT THIS SPONGE.
I SAW IT ON *IT'S MORNING.*
WE CAME ALL THE WAY OUT TO TACHIKAWA FOR A *SINGLE* SPONGE?
IT IS CUTE, THOUGH.
I FEEL BAD. IT'S LIKE I MADE HER COME OUT HERE.
EVEN WHEN SHE'S NOT FEELING WELL, WAKO-CHAN SMILES.
I HAVE TO BE STRONG...
HAAH...
MEGURU-KUN, IF YOU'RE GOING TO SIGH, DO IT WHILE SITTING IN THIS CHAIR.

THE ONLY SON OF A WEALTHY FAMILY.
THE UNIVERSITY STUDENT WHO LIVES WITH HIS GRAND-MOTHER BY THE SEA.
YOU WANTED LOTS OF SPACE FOR YOUR FIRST APARTMENT, SO YOU MOVED TO A PLACE TWENTY MINUTES FROM THE NEAREST STATION, AND NOW YOU HAVE REGRETS.
THIS SET LOOKS GOOD, TOO!
......

A KITCHEN WHERE SOMEONE IS LIKELY TO MAKE FANCY FRUIT SALAD FOR SUPPER!
A SOFA AN AMERICAN WOULD EAT POPCORN ON WHILE WATCHING MOVIES!
A DOLL THAT I DON'T KNOW WHAT IT IS!
A DOG...
AND...
OKAY, MAYBE I'LL GET THIS!
I WANT TO MAKE HER EVEN HAPPIER!
EVERY-THING I'VE GOT!
SQUEEEEZE
JUST LIKE THAT, WAKO-CHAN'S ELECTRIC.
RIGHT. MAYBE I CAN MAKE HER TEAR UP.
KYAA!
KYAA!

NO. THE HOUSE IS FULL OF THINGS LIKE THAT.

MORE STUFF MAKES CLEANING A NIGHT-MARE.
YOU'RE SO PRACTICAL SOMETIMES, WAKO-CHAN.
OH, BUT...
A COVER OR SOMETHING'S OKAY--LIKE THIS.

I DUNNO ABOUT THE COLOR.

YOU DON'T LIKE IT?
I'M JUST NOT SURE IT'LL GO WITH THE REST OF THE HOUSE.
LIKE THE CURTAINS, THE FLOOR...
OVERALL AESTHETIC, HUH?

HMM.

HANG ON A SEC!
THERE'S A KNIFE RACK!
WHOA, INTERNATIONAL.
THEY'RE CHEAP. HOW ABOUT WE GET SOME OF THESE CONTAINERS?
AND STORAGE BAGS. AND HANGERS.
WE DON'T NORMALLY USE NAPKINS, BUT THESE ARE ADORABLE!
Ikeya Restaurant and Café
OH! SOMETHING SMELLS GOOD.
LET'S GET SOMETHING TO EAT!
IKEYA

WHUMP
I'M EXHAUSTED!

EVEN IN A PLACE LIKE THIS, WE'RE ONLY BUYING SMALL THINGS.
IT'S HARD TO MAKE BIG PURCHASES.
BUT IT'S FUN TO LOOK AROUND. AND GOOD EXERCISE!

REMEMBER MY KOUHAI WE RAN INTO IN GINZA?
SHE ASKED IF WE'RE MOVING TO SHIBUYA.
HUNH. WHY SHIBUYA?
RIGHT? I WONDER.

I THOUGHT IT WAS FUNNY, SO I DIDN'T TELL HER.
MAYBE SHE GOT CARRIED AWAY WITH THE IDEA OF MOVING AND THAT'S WHY WE'RE AT IKEYA?
MAKES SENSE.

AH, IT'S NO GOOD. I'M GONNA FALL ASLEEP HERE.
SAME.
NEXT TIME WE COME, LET'S DECIDE IN ADVANCE WHAT WE'RE GOING TO BUY.
I MEAN, IT *DOES* MEAN COMING ALL THE WAY OUT TO TACHI-KAWA.
TRUE.
......
BLINK
ぱちっ

DUUN

WE'LL TAKE IT.

WE'LL DELIVER IT NEXT WEEK. IS THAT ALL RIGHT?
YES.
HOW WOULD YOU LIKE TO PAY?
CREDIT CARD.
BA-DMP BA-DMP

THANK YOU VERY MUCH!
BA-DMP
BA-DMP BA-DMP
BA-DMP

WE ACTUALLY BOUGHT IT...
THAT SORT OF PLACE IS ALL ABOUT IMPULSE BUYS.
WE'LL HAVE TO GET RID OF THE OLD SOFA BEFORE THE NEW ONE ARRIVES.

WHEN IS BIG GARBAGE DAY?
DO EITHER OF US HAVE THE DAY OFF?
I WONDER IF THE DOOR'S WIDE ENOUGH...
WILL IT FIT IN THE ELEVATOR?

WE CAN RETURN IT IF IT DOESN'T FIT, RIGHT?
AH, STOP IT!
IT'S FINE! IT WAS A GOOD BUY!
I KNOW! JUST BLAME IT ON ME!
WE BOUGHT ON MY LITTLE WHIM!
OKAY?

BUT...

IT'D BE PRETTY HOT IF I LOUNGED ON IT AFTER GETTING OUT OF THE BATH, RIGHT?
SO HOT...
NOW WE NEED A BIG, FLUFFY ROBE AND SOME DECORATIVE PLANTS.
LET'S STOP IN AT NISETAN!
OKAY-- BUT NO MORE IMPULSE BUYS!

mmggling
Got a new sofa! I wish I could live at IKEYA.
BA-TNK
KA-CHAK
PERFECT.
OH! WAKO-CHAN, YOU'RE HOME!

YOU DON'T CHANGE, EVEN WITH A NEW SOFA.

The Eighth One
10:00
ALARM
SNOOZE
BEEP BEEP BEEP BEEP
BEEP BEEP BEEP BEEP
SNUG SNUG
ゴソゴソ
BEEP
8
LINE
2
6
BEFORE SHE DOES ANYTHING ELSE...
MACHIDA WAKO STARTS HER MORNING...

10:03
100%
SaftBank
MEGURU-KUN
ARCH
BY CHECKING SOCIAL MEDIA.
My Androgynous Boyfriend
The Eighth One

Meguru-kun's too cute
The world's at peace

button alone is not eno
RT to spread the word!

Meguru-kun, my standby s
so when I wake up in the
work is good, my boyfrien
maybe win the lottery

KIRAMEGU
SECRET SHOT
uess they've been datin
not hiding it. This
agency also gave the ok
the other day at Yonto
proud, so the lack of in
reminds me, on Insta
IKEYA...move
Oh!
This is for sure
So happy for them
the best, so with this
went on a date in Gin
......
......

WHAAT? ME AND KIRA-KUN?!
WHERE DID THAT COME FROM?!

THEY'RE SAYING YOU'VE BEEN CLOSE FOR A WHILE NOW.
AND THAT YOU SAID SOMETHING AT YONTO THE OTHER DAY?
OH... I SAID I HAD A LOVER...
AND THEN THE NAIL THING.
WE ALWAYS GET OUR NAILS DONE TOGETHER.

NO, THEY SAID YOU HAVE A HEART DESIGN ON YOUR LEFT RING FINGER, SO.
WHAAAT?!
THIS
INSTA.
AND TWITTER.
AND, WELL, WE GOT THAT NEW COUCH. THE TIMING'S PERFECT.
SO THEY'RE MAKING ASSUMPTIONS, YOU KNOW?
NGH... THEY ARE...
WOW...
PLUS THE BOSS SAID SOMETHING SIMILAR...
AND THEN THERE'S THE FACT THAT KIRA-KUN ONLY LIKES YOUR TWEETS.
BECAUSE I'M HIS ONLY FRIEND...
......

LISTEN!
I'LL SAY THIS RIGHT NOW! THERE'S NOTHING BETWEEN ME AND KIRA-KUN!
YOU'RE THE ONLY ONE FOR ME, WAKO-CHAN!
DON'T WORRY ABOUT ANY OF IT!

I KNOW THAT, SO IT DOESN'T MATTER WHAT ANYONE ELSE SAYS.

STILL, IT'S KINDA FUNNY! THEY HAVE SUCH POWERFUL IMAGINATIONS!

SWOON

Wako-chan...

RIGHT. YES. EXACTLY!

I'M GOING TO WORK, OKAY?!

KISS

EEE!

Café Renoair

Café Renoair

SO HOW LONG HAVE YOU TWO BEEN DATING?

WHAT...?

OH! WAS THAT TOO FORWARD? I'M SORRY!
HOW LONG HAVE YOU TWO BEEN *FRIENDS*?
UH, FRIENDS?
WHY WOULD I REMEMBER THAT?

IT'S VERY IMPORTANT.
THIS INTERVIEW IS ABOUT BEAUTIFUL BOYS.
THEN I'LL ANSWER.
PLAN TO INCREASE FEMALE READERSHIP

WE'RE AT THE SAME AGENCY...
BUT KIRA-KUN'S MODELED SINCE HE WAS A KID.
I JOINED LATER.
A COINCIDENCE THEN?
YES.
A SCOUT DISCOVERED ME WHILE I WAS WORKING AT A SHOP IN HARAJUKU.
I WAS SUSPICIOUS AT FIRST--ON GUARD.

SO YOU JOINED BECAUSE YOU ADORED KIRA-SAN...
WHAT? IS THAT TRUE?
NO, IT WAS MORE NUANCED THAN--

SO HOW DID YOU GET SO CLOSE?
OH! THAT'S A FUNNY STORY.
FOR SOME REASON, KIRA-KUN WAS WANDERING AROUND WHEN I WENT TO THE STUDIO FOR MY FIRST SHOOT.
IT'S SMALL, BUT I GOT LOST. I HAD NO CLUE WHERE TO GO.

LATER, I REALIZED KIRA-KUN HADN'T NOTICED ANYONE BUT ME--
SO IT WAS LOVE AT FIRST SIGHT FOR KIRA-SAN.
I GUESS SO?
?
WH... WHAT'S HAPPEN-ING?

BLINK
ぱっ
RIGHT. I'VE GOT WAKO-CHAN.
I DON'T CARE HOW THEY INTERPRET MY FRIEND-SHIP WITH KIRA-KUN.
SHE SAID IT'S OKAY. AND I MEAN, THESE LITTLE DETAILS...
SO IN THE SPECIAL INTERVIEW YOU GAVE THE OTHER DAY...
YOU SAID YOU WANTED THE PERSON YOU LOVE TO ADMIRE YOU.
WERE YOU TALKING ABOUT KIRA-SAN?

WERE YOU?
HEY. I'M SPEAKING TO YOU.
HELLOOO?
GRIT
きゅっ
...

NO, I WASN'T.
I WAS TALKING ABOUT THE PERSON I'M DATING RIGHT NOW.
TNK
I'M GOING OUT WITH WAKO-CHAN.
MEGURU-SAN...

WHAT SHOULD WE DO?
EDIT THAT PART OUT?
WHAT ABOUT REPLACING "WAKO-CHAN" WITH "LOVER"?
RIGHT...

MAKE IT VAGUE SO IT CAN BE TAKEN EITHER WAY.
WHAAAT ?!

WHATEVER... WAKO-CHAN WILL UNDER-STAND...

LIKE A DOG WITH A BONE HERE.
TNK

MEGURU SAID HE'S WITH WAKO.

HE AND I ARE NOT DATING.

PERIOD.

I HAVE NEVER DATED ANYONE.
MY BODY AND SOUL ARE PURE.

THAT EDITOR GOT REALLY WORKED UP TOWARD THE END, HUH?
YOU REALLY DON'T MIND IF I PUT THIS IN AN ARTICLE?!
THANK YOU SO MUCH!!
WHAT WAS THAT ASSIGNMENT ANYWAY?
I WONDER WHAT THE ARTICLE WILL BE LIKE?
THANKS, KIRA-KUN...

I'M GLAD WE'RE FRIENDS.
YOU WOULD BE.
WE'RE BEST FRIENDS, HUH?
IS THAT WHAT WE ARE?
YUP.

The Ninth One
AH, IT'S RAINING.
THE SKY'S CLEARING UP, THOUGH. IT'LL STOP SOON...
YOU'RE CATCHING A CAB-- RIGHT, KIRA-KUN?
WHAT ABOUT YOU?
DUNNO. MAYBE I'LL BUY AN UMBRELLA.
SUN SHOWERS ARE NICE, HUH?
I'VE ALWAYS LIKED THINGS THAT GLITTER WHEN LIGHT HITS THEM.
GLASS, LACE CURTAINS.
MY MOTHER'S MAKEUP KIT.
ACCESSORIES.

IT STARTED WITH THAT SORT OF THING.
I'LL LISTEN UNTIL THE RAIN STOPS...
SO TELL ME HOW YOU AND WAKO MET.
HUH?
WELL... IT WAS THIS TIME OF YEAR...
I'D JUST STARTED HIGH SCHOOL...

My Androgynous Boyfriend
The Ninth One
I'M SOUMA MEGURU, GRADE TEN, CLASS B.

I'M NOT ASKING YOUR NAME.

WHAT'S WITH THIS GETUP?

THE HAIR.

IF I DON'T WEAR IT LONG, I CAN'T TIE IT BACK IN AN UPDO.

AND THE GIRL'S NECKTIE?

MY SKIN HAS COOL UNDERTONES. PINK LOOKS BETTER ON ME.

AND THE SOCKS?

A SPLASH OF COLOR...

SHUT UP!

YOU'RE ONLY A TENTH GRADER! Y'KNOW WHAT HAPPENS WHEN YOU ACT LIKE THAT?!

DON'T! YOU'RE GOING TO WRINKLE MY SHIRT!

STOP IT.

I CAN'T BELIEVE IT, OUT HERE IN THE MIDDLE OF NO-WHERE...

THROUGH SOME GENETIC MIRACLE...

HUH...?

UH, UM...

LIKE A SHINING STAR.

NOT A PLANET, A STAR.

ER... UM.

WHO ARE YOU...?

I HEARD RUMORS, BUT I NEVER DREAMED...

TCH! MACHIDA? LET'S GET OUT OF HERE.

SHE'S TOO MUCH TROUBLE.

WHAT?! HEY! PLEASE HELP ME!!

YOU!!

EEP!

GRAB

I'M SORRY! I'M NOT LIKE OTHER PEOPLE!!

YOU ARE THE ABSOLUTE CUTEST!
HUH?
THAT'S HOW I MET WAKO-CHAN.
IN A SMALL TOWN IN NORTHERN KANTO...
THE SORT OF PLACE WHERE EVERYONE GOES TO A●N ON THE WEEKENDS.
SORRY.
I'VE NEVER BEEN ABLE TO RESIST ANYTHING CUTE OR PRETTY.
SO... YOU LIKE MAKEUP AND FASHION TOO, MACHIDA-SENPAI?

Idol-loving Wako.

HEY! WHY DON'T YOU GIVE IT A TRY, SOUMA-KUN?
YOU KNOW, THIS SORT OF THING.
HUH-- ME?
I MEAN, YOU'RE SO CUTE. IT'D BE A SHAME IF YOU DIDN'T.
CUTE THINGS MAKE THE WORLD BETTER.
OH, BUT I'M NOT--
LET'S SHOW THEM! MAKE THE WORLD BETTER!
BUT THE EQUIP-MENT...
NO WORRIES. I HAVE SOME AT MY HOUSE.
EDITING, THOUGH ...
I'LL DO ALL OF THAT STUFF.
Moving right along.
VRRR

REC
JUST BE YOURSELF, SOUMA-KUN.

WEAR WHAT YOU WANT, PUT ON MAKEUP.
LAUGH...
TALK...
HAVE FUN!

SEARCH
soon, with a little chitchat.
Meguru-kun! You're super cute
again today! Tomorrow, schoo
I love it
I'm so happy you've been
posting so much.
I want to be you, Meguru-
kun. I'm doing makeup
You're the absolute cu
Tell me what brands
Whoa. You're so coo
your hair is
cute
ek of spring outfits

SEARCH
WE SAW YOUR VIDEO, MEGURU-KUN!
YOU'RE GETTING SO MANY FOLLOW-ERS!
YOU'RE SUPER POPULAR!
YOU HAVE TO TELL US WHAT MAKEUP YOU USE!
Another cute day
I ended up com
see you again to
too cute, exactly
my thing.
want to see tha
routine.
I love how you
talk, too. Cute!
tching the vid
makes me ha
Cute
TCH!
WHOA!
SORRY, I GOTTA GO!
LIBRARY
KLATTA

MACHIDA-SENPAI.
THANKS FOR EDITING THE VIDEOS.
BECAUSE OF YOU, I'M ACTUALLY MAKING FRIENDS!
SEE? I TOLD YOU.
BUT YOU DON'T NEED TO WORRY ABOUT ME. GO SOCIALIZE.
HUH? BUT...
I DO IT BECAUSE I LIKE IT.
I WANT TO WORK IN THIS FIELD SOMEDAY.
YOU KNOW-- SHARING AWESOME THINGS WITH PEOPLE.
I'M THINKING OF TRYING FOR A UNIVERSITY IN TOKYO.
WHAT? *WOW!* TOKYO!
HARA-JUKU! SHIBUYA!
RIGHT.

I BET THERE'S A *TON* OF SHINY THINGS THERE.

I WANT TO BE WITH SOMEONE WHO SHINES.
HUH?
SHF

SO
WHO--?

IT WAS A LONG TIME UNTIL I GRADUATED.
AFTERWARD, I CAME STRAIGHT TO TOKYO...
WHICH BRINGS US TO NOW.

I HOPE THINGS ARE GOING WELL, BUT I NEED THAT MANU-SCRIPT!!!
OH! ANOTHER HOUR?! I'LL BE WAITING!!!!
IS THE PRINTER STILL GOOD?!
FLAP
BRRRING
I'M PROOFING!
BR
THE FORMAT'S WRONG! AND WE'RE MISSING A PAGE!
TMP TMP
RRRING
PI-POON~!
TMP
DID WE HEAR BACK FROM THE DESIGNER YET?!
KLATTA
BRRRI
WHAT?! THE FLU?!
My Androgynous Boyfriend
The Tenth One
FINIIISH-ED!!

Editorial department on proofreading day.
ばた…
FLOP
HURRY! WE HAVE TO MAKE IT TO YOKOHAMA ARENA IN TIME!
YOU HAVE THE PEN LIGHTS?!
バタ
TMP
バタ
TMP
バタ
TMP
…
…
I CAN'T GO ON. I'LL NEVER MOVE AGAIN.
I NEED A NAP. I'M DEAD. I'M SO TIRED, I COULD DIE.
THOSE KIDS ARE TOO MUCH...
PIRON~!
Meguru-kun
What time do you think you'll make it home?
SHWMP
OH! YOU'RE UP.

WE'VE MISSED EACH OTHER ALL WEEK. I SHOULD PICK UP SOME CAKE ON MY WAY HOME.
THE CHEESE KIND MEGURU-KUN LIKES.
SURPRISE HIM, AT LEAST...

BE PRESENT-ABLE, AT LEAST.
FIX MY MAKEUP, AT LEAST.
SMILE, AT LEAST.

OKAY!
SMILE

I'M HOME!

WELCOME HOOOME!
SHWP
SHWP
TA-DAA! SURPRISED?
TODAY'S THE SEVENTH ANNIVERSARY OF US DATING!
SEE? LOOK!
I MADE ALL YOUR FAVORITE FOODS, WAKO-CHAN.
AND HERE! A PRESENT.
Photo Book

RIGHT... TODAY'S...
OUR ANNIVER-SARY...

I CAN'T...
ドザッ
FWMP

WOW. I LOVE YOU, BUT I DIDN'T DO ANY-THING.
YOU DO EVERYTHING FOR ME, AND I NEVER GIVE BACK.
I WORK ALL THE TIME. I ONLY THINK OF MYSELF.
I'M SO *SELFISH*, A TOTAL DISASTER OF A PERSON.

わっ
WAH!
I CAN'T ANYMORE! I JUST CAN'T! I'M TOO MUCH OF A DISASTER!
OH! THIS CAKE'S FROM THAT SHOP NEAR THE STATION.
YOU BOUGHT IT FOR *MEEE!*

I LOVE, LOVE, LOVE YOU.
I'M SO GLAD WE'VE BEEN TOGETHER ALL THIS TIME.
THANK YOU.

ME TOO.
JUST BEING WITH YOU MAKES ME HAPPY.
I LOVE YOU.
MEGURU-KUN...

WHUP
BLUSH
YAAAY!
KYAA!
SQUEEEEEZE
WAH!
KISS
EHEH HEH HEH...
KISS
KISS

MM...
YOU REALLY HAVE TOMORROW OFF?
YEAH. PROOF-READING'S DONE. ALL SET.

GOOD.
WE CAN SLEEP IN FOR ONCE.
SHFF

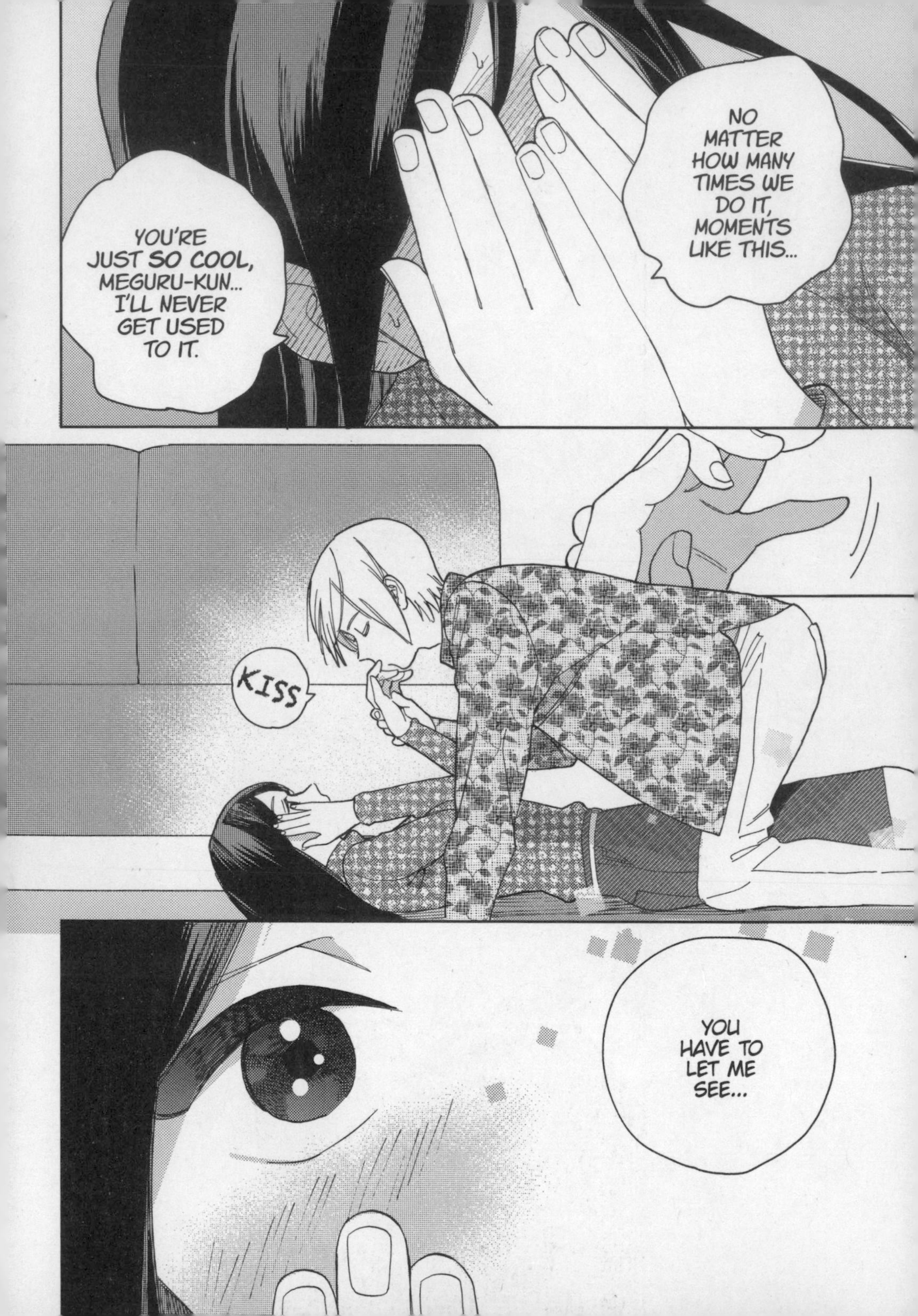
NO MATTER HOW MANY TIMES WE DO IT, MOMENTS LIKE THIS...
YOU'RE JUST SO COOL, MEGURU-KUN... I'LL NEVER GET USED TO IT.
KISS
YOU HAVE TO LET ME SEE...

THE CUTEST PERSON IN THE WORLD.

PURURURURU♪
EDITORIAL
PURURURURU♪
EDITORIAL
BIP
SORRY, MACHIDA-SAN!
COULD YOU COME INTO THE OFFICE FOR A MINUTE? IT'S ABOUT THAT MANUSCRIPT.
I'M REALLY SORRY!
WAKO-CHAN, WAKO-CHAN.
MMM.
THAT CALL SOUNDED URGENT.
MMM.

JUST FIVE MORE MINUTES...
YOU'RE HOPELESS...
GOT YOUR PHONE? ALL CHARGED UP?
YEP!
WALLET?
YEP!
MAKEUP?

GET OUT THERE THEN!